PAINES PLOUGH and **TRAVERSE THEATRE COMPANY** present

HELMET

by **Douglas Maxwell**

First performed at the Traverse Theatre 8 March 2002

painesPLOUGH

TRAVERSE
THEATRE

HELMET

by **Douglas Maxwell**

Cast

Ameet Chana Sal
Tommy Mullins Roddy aka Helmet

Director John Tiffany
Designer Neil Warmington
Lighting Designer Natasha Chivers
Sound Designer Brian Docherty for scientific support dept.
Movement Director Allan Irvine
Digital Animation Arts In Motion

Traverse

Stage Manager Gavin Harding
Deputy Stage Manager Pauline Wood
Assistant Stage Manager Mickey Brendan

On Tour

Company Stage Manager Pauline Wood
Technical Stage Manager Maria Bechaalani

Author's Note

I wrote *Helmet* during a particularly bleak time in my life. That's typical for me though. Every time I'm moping about miserable, talking about death to barbers and telling people I'm giving up, I'll write something which reminds me just how much fun it all is. I write myself out of trouble right at the last minute and I haven't got a clue how I do it.

Maybe it's the simple process of spending so much time in a fantasy world which cheers me up. Or just my essert mind which clamps up tight when I'm happy and solvent but somehow springs into life when it's been brooding for a while. I dunno.

But in 1996 when I'd been unemployed for a year and a half I wrote *Decky Does A Bronco*. And last year, when my little brush with success had sucked away my last few drops of creativity, I wrote a history play called *James II* which got me all excited and buzzing again. The trouble is, I might not be able to do it the next time. What if the great idea which swoops in and saves the day doesn't come? That's the worry. But one thing for sure, in 1998 at the Performing Arts Lab in Kent, it arrived. Just in time.

I had been working in a computer games shop in Shawlands for too long. My dream of being a playwright which was noble in the first few years had crossed the line into being embarrassing and was now just sad. I sent away my latest script to the usuals and got the usual response. If slightly worse. It was time to give up.

Then, out of the blue, I was invited to attend a workshop week for writers in Kent called PAL. TAG had sent in an old script of mine, *Decky Does A Bronco*, which had been knocking about their office for years and it got picked. The only thing on my mind at that time was the shop, the games we sold and the people who bought them. So I blagged my way into PAL with a half baked idea about a boy who steals money to buy a game.

I was inspired at PAL. By the tutors and other writers. With their help *Helmet* became a complicatedly structured piece, modelled on computer games, about a wee boy whose real life is so cold and awful that he quite happily plays games to get away from it.

And maybe that's why I love the story so much. When your real life sucks, what's so wrong about disappearing into a fantasy if you can find one? Maybe Helmet, the boy in the play, goes too far in, but I forgive him. I do it too. I hide in The New Play which has dropped in from nowhere and pretend that the real, nasty stuff isn't happening. It stops me giving up. And I think we all need something which stops us giving up.

Douglas Maxwell
February 2002

The Company

Douglas Maxwell Writer

Douglas Maxwell was born in 1974 in Girvan, a small town on the Ayrshire coast of Scotland.

He is the author of many plays including *Decky Does A Bronco* and *Our Bad Magnet*. *Our Bad Magnet* was Douglas Maxwell's first play and was staged at the Tron Theatre Glasgow in 2000 and then revived in 2001 as a co-production with Borderline. The revival played The Assembly Rooms in Edinburgh during the festival and then embarked on a large scale tour of Scotland. *Decky Does A Bronco* was first performed in 2000 by Grid Iron Theatre Company winning a Fringe First, The Stage Award and nominated for The Barclay Card Stage Award 2001 for Best Touring Production. It toured nationwide, including two national tours of Scotland, a major English tour including three weeks in London's Almeida Theatre and an Irish tour.

Douglas has three new plays in the pipeline: *The Ballad of James II* for the Tron, *Variety* for Grid Iron and *Melody* for the Traverse.

Arts In Motion Digital Animation

Operating in Theatrical and Multimedia Productions and Services since 1985, the company offers performances, workshops, set design and build, short films and animation, video documentation and graphic design. It has a long history of work with children under its touring identity as The Crown Jewels and more recently Cartoon Theatre. Most recently it's film and video work has attracted attention and praise. A Highland Festival commissioned piece *Elements* recently toured the Highlands with the Rob Hall Jazz band and the company has worked on film with dance most recently with Laura Steckler, Ruby Worth and Caroline Reagh.

Ameet Chana Sal

For Paines Plough: *Crazyhorse*. Other theatre work includes: *Papa Was a Bus Conductor Innit* (Lyric Hammersmith); *Bollywood 2000* (RIFCO); *Balti Kings* (Tamasha); *Don't Look At My Sisters…Innit!* (One Nation); *Arrange That Marriage* (Tabularasa); *Ready Or Not* (Stratford East); *Skeleton* (Soho Theatre); *Wicked! Yaar* (National Theatre); *Ungrateful Dead; Bad Company; Girlies* (all Watermans); *East Is East* (Royal Court Workshop); *An Immigrants Song* (Cars in Water); *Voices in the Wind* (RNT).

Television work includes: *Goodbye Mr Steadman* (Alibi); *League of Gentlemen; Roger Roger; The Accused* (all BBC).

Film includes: *Bend It Like Beckham* (Bilb Prods) released spring 2002 and *Wild West* (Film Four).

Natasha Chivers Lighting Designer

For Paines Plough: *Tiny Dynamite* (also Frantic Assembly, Contact); *Crazy Gary's Mobile Disco* (also Sgript Cymru). For the Traverse: *Among Unbroken Hearts* (also Bush Theatre).

Other work includes: *Yiimimangaliso - The Mysteries* At Wiltons Music Hall (Broomhill/Spier Festival, S.Africa); *Notre Dame de Paris* (Strathcona Theatre Co - tour/Lyric, Hammersmith); *A Listening Heaven* (Royal Lyceum Theatre, Edinburgh); *1001 Nights* and *The Firebird* (Unicorn Theatre Co.); *Orfeo*, (Opera North); *Hymns* and *Sell Out* (Frantic Assembly). Site specific work includes; *Ghost Ward* and *Into Our Dreams* (Almeida Theatre Co), *Mincemeat* at The Old Hartley's Jam Factory (Cardboard Citizens); *Mapping the Edge* (Wilson Wilson Co); *The Salt Garden* (Strathcona at the National Maritime Museum; Greenwich) *Waving* (Oily Cart in Hydro-therapy pools/tour).

Future work includes: *A Chaste Maid in Cheapside* (Almeida Theatre Co); *Peepshow*, a new musical from Frantic Assembly.

Brian Docherty for scientific support dept. Composer

For the Traverse: *Among Unbroken Hearts.* Other work includes: *Stroma, Othello* (TAG) and *Macbeth* (Awarehaus Theatre Company). Collaborations with: Daddy's Favourite, Adventures In Stereo, Mount Vernon Arts Lab., This Mortal Coil, Vic Goddard.
www.scientificsupportdept.com

Allan Irvine Movement Director

Allan is from Stirling and began B-Boying (Hip Hop dance styles) in 1984. He was soon conned into contemporary. After leaving school at 16 he became a Youth Trainee in dance with Stirling Council and went on to study dance at Dundee College and Northern School of Contemporary Dance (Leeds). Allan has worked for Dundee Rep Community Dance Team, Cois Ceim (Dublin), Dundee College, Telford College and has been Dance Artist in Residence at City Moves (Aberdeen), MacRobert Arts Centre (Stirling) and is currently Youth Dance Action Researcher at Dance Base. He also directs and performs in his company Freshness.

Tommy Mullins Roddy aka Helmet

Tommy graduated from RSAMD in 2000.

Work includes: For the Traverse: *King of the Fields*; *Dr Korczak's Example* (TAG); *Damaged Goods* (Tron); *Sunset Song* (Prime Productions Scottish Tour); *The Reader* (Borderline Theatre); *Cinderella* (Scottish Ballet); *Twelfth Night* and *Hamlet* (both SYT); *Have You Seen This Girl* (National Youth Theatre) and *Just One More Dance* (Glasgow City Council).

For television: *Inspector Rebus* (ITV)

John Tiffany Director

Trained: Glasgow University. Associate Director at Paines Plough since October 2001. Literary Director at the Traverse from 1997 to 2001. For the Traverse: *Gagarin Way* by Gregory Burke (also RNT and Arts Theatre); *Among Unbroken Hearts* by Henry Adam (also Bush); *Abandonment* by Kate Atkinson; *King Of The Fields* by Stuart Paterson; *The Juju Girl* by Aileen Ritchie; *Danny 306 + Me (4 Ever)* by David Greig (also Birmingham Rep); *Perfect Days* by Liz Lochhead (also Hampstead, Vaudeville and tour); *Greta* by James Duthie and *Passing Places* by Stephen Greenhorn (also Citizens' and tour). Other work includes *Grimm Tales* (Leicester Haymarket) and *The Sunset Ship* (Young Vic). Film includes: *Karmic Mothers* (BBC Tartan Shorts) and *Golden Wedding* (BBC Two Lives).

Neil Warmington Designer

For Paines Plough: *Splendour*, *Riddance*; *Crazyhorse*. For Traverse Theatre: *Gagarin Way*; *Wiping My Mother's Arse*; *Family*; *Passing Places*; *King of the Fields*; *Full Moon for a Solemn Mass* (also Barbican Pit). Other work includes: *Marriage of Figaro* (Garsington Opera); *Desire Under the Elms*; *Jane Eyre* (Shared Experience); *Ghosts*; *Love's Labours Lost*; *Don Juan*; *The Taming of the Shrew* (English Touring Theatre); *Dissent*; *Angels in America* (7:84); *Woyzeck*; *The Glass Menagerie*; *Comedians* (Royal Lyceum, Edinburgh); *Life is a Dream*; *Fiddler on the Roof* (West Yorkshire Playhouse); *The Duchess of Malfi* (Bath Theatre Royal); *Henry V* (Royal Shakespeare Company); *Much Ado About Nothing* (Queen's, London); *The Life of Stuff* (Donmar Warehouse); *Much Ado about Nothing*; *Waiting For Godot* (Liverpool Everyman); *The Tempest* (Contact, Manchester); *Women Laughing* (Watford); *Troilus & Cressida* (Opera North); *Oedipus Rex* (Connecticut State Opera). Awards include: 3 TMA Awards for best design (*Life is a Dream*; *Passing Places*; *Jane Eyre*); The Linbury Prize for Stage Design and The Sir Alfred Munnings Florence Prize for painting.

Paines Plough

The driving force behind Paines Plough is the vision of the playwright and the company has been discovering outstanding new voices in British theatre since 1974. Funded by the Arts Council of England we seek, encourage, develop, support and produce writers nation-wide, touring a minimum of two new plays a year throughout the UK and presenting regular rehearsed readings by writers with varying levels of experience.

In 1997, Paines Plough appointed its sixth Artistic Director, Vicky Featherstone. Since Vicky's appointment, Paines Plough has gone from strength to strength making iself one of the most respected theatre companies in Britain today.

At every level, writers are encouraged to be courageous in their work, to challenge our notions of theatre and the society we live in.

Since 1997 Paines Plough has produced: *Tiny Dynamite* by Abi Morgan (MEN Best Fringe Production), *Crazy Gary's Mobile Disco* by Gary Owen, *Splendour* by Abi Morgan (TMA Barclays Theatre Award Best Play and Best Director, Fringe First and a Herald Angel 2000), *Riddance* by Linda McLean, (Fringe First and a Herald Angel 1999), *The Cosmonaut's Last Message to the Woman He Once Loved in the Former Soviet Union* by David Greig, *Crave* by Sarah Kane, *Sleeping Around* by Hilary Fannin, Stephen Greenhorn, Abi Morgan and Mark Ravenhill, *Crazyhorse* by Parv Bancil and *The Wolves* by Michael Punter.

Education Work Paines Plough offers a variety of workshops and teaching materials to accompany *Helmet*. If you would like more information on education work please contact Susannah on 020 72404533 or go to the Paines Plough Website at www.painesplough.com.

Wild Lunch Wild Lunch is a regular Paines Plough festival of script-in-hand performances, born out of a selected writers group, the latest, Wild Lunch VI is a co-production with Graeae Theatre Company and will culminate in a festival in June 2002.

This Other England Paines Plough has been awarded the Peggy Ramsay Theatre Company of the Year 2001 for *This Other England*. The commissions are Simon Armitage, Biyi Bandele, David Greig, Linda McLean, Abi Morgan, Philip Ridley, Peter Straughan, Naomi Wallace and Enda Walsh. The plays written for *This Other England* will share the theme of the development of the English language over the last thousand years. Our ambition is for the nine plays to create an alternative census of Britain at the beginning of the twenty-first century.

Paines Plough Company

Artistic Director Vicky Featherstone
Associate Director John Tiffany
General Manager Caroline Newall
Literary Associate Lucy Morrison
Admin Assistant Susannah Matthews

Board of Directors

Roanna Benn, Tamara Cizeika, Ian Codrington (Company Secretary), Giles Croft, David Edwards (Chair), Chris Elwell (Vice Chair), Jenny Sealey

Paines Plough are supported by:

Are you on Paines Plough's mailing list?

If you would like to be on Paines Plough's free mailing list please call, email or post your details to:

Susannah Matthews
Paines Plough
4th Floor
43 Aldwych
London
WC2B 4DN
Tel + 00 44 (0) 20 7240 4533
office@painesplough.com

Traverse Theatre

Artistic Director Philip Howard

The Traverse is Scotland's new writing theatre. Founded in 1963 by a group of maverick artists and enthusiasts, it began as an imaginative attempt to capture the spirit of adventure and experimentation of the Edinburgh Festival all year round. Throughout the decades, the Traverse has evolved and grown in artistic output and ambition. It has refined its mission by strengthening its commitment to producing new plays by Scottish and international playwrights and actively nurturing them throughout their careers. Traverse productions have been seen world-wide and tour regularly throughout the UK and overseas.

The Traverse has produced over 600 new plays in its lifetime and, through a spirit of innovation and risk-taking, has launched the careers of many of the country's best known writers. From, among others, Stanley Eveling in the 1960s, John Byrne in the 1970s, Liz Lochhead in the 1980s, David Greig in the 1990s to Gregory Burke in the 2000s, the Traverse is unique in Scotland in its dedication to new writing. It fulfils the crucial role of providing the infrastructure, professional support and expertise to ensure the development of a dynamic theatre culture for Scotland.

The Traverse's activities encompass every aspect of playwriting and production, providing and facilitating play-reading panels, script development workshops, rehearsed readings, public playwriting workshops, writers' groups, a public playwrights' platform, The Monday Lizard, discussions and special events. The Traverse's work with young people is of supreme importance and takes the form of encouraging playwriting through its flagship education project, Class Act, as well as the Traverse Young Writers Group.

"Edinburgh's Traverse Theatre is a mini-festival in itself"
The Times

From its conception in the 1960s, the Traverse has remained a pivotal venue during the Edinburgh Festival. It receives enormous critical and audience acclaim for its programming, as well as regularly winning awards.

The year 2001 was no different, with the Traverse being awarded two Scotsman Fringe Firsts and two Herald Angels for its own productions *Gagarin Way* and *Wiping My Mother's Arse* and a Herald Archangel for overall artistic excellence.

Traverse Theatre Company

Gillian Adams Second Chef
Jeremy Adderley Bar Café Manager
Louise Anderson Marketing & Press Assistant
Paul Axford Corporate Development Co-Ordinator
Maria Bechaalani Deputy Electrician
Andy Catlin Marketing Manager
David Connell Finance Manager
Andrew Coulton Assistant Electrician
Eric Dickinson Third Chef
Jude Durnan Deputy Box Office Manager
Lynn Ferguson Wardrobe Supervisor
Michael Fraser Theatre Manager
David Freeburn Box Office Manager
Mike Griffiths Administrative Producer
Jayne Gross Development Manager
Kellie Harris Head Chef
David Henderson Bar Café Attendant
Philip Howard Artistic Director
Hal Jones Carpenter
Mark Leese Design Associate
Kevin McCune Assistant Bar Café Manager
Catherine MacNeil Adminstrator
Katherine Mendelsohn International Literary Associate
Kate Nelson Monday Lizard Co-ordinator
Duncan Nicoll Deputy Bar Café Manager
Lara McDonald Administrative Assistant
Nick Miller Production Manager
Helen-Marie O'Malley Assistant Director
Pauleen Rafferty Finance & Personnel Assistant
Renny Robertson Chief Electrician
Hannah Rye Literary Development Officer
Kathryn Sawers Bar Café Supervisor
Roxana Silbert Literary Director
Zoe Squair Front of House Manager
Stephanie Thorburn Wardrobe Assistant
Jenni Wardle Marketing & Press Officer
Douglas White Temporary Finance Assistant
Isabel Wright SAC Playwright In Residence

Working for the Traverse

Ewan Anderson, Nancy Birch, Charlie Campbell, Anna Copland, Neil Coull, Annie Divine, Ben Ewart-Dean, Linda Gunn, Nathan Huxtable, David Inverarity, Chris Jones, Amy Logan, John Lyndon, Euan MacDonald, Stuart McDonald, Donna McGlynn, Catriona MacInnes, Eleanor Macleod, Daniel Mackie, Clare Padgett, Carlos Perdices Cuesta, Fionn Petch, Helen Pidd, Dominic Rafferty, Naomi Richards, Naomi Schwock, Alison Macleod, Alistair Stott, John Thompson, Neil West, Anna Wetz.

Traverse Theatre Board of Directors

Stuart Hepburn (Chair), Kate Atkinson, Steven Cotton, Leslie Evans, Geraldine Gammell, Robin Harper MSP, Christine Hamilton, John Stone, Stuart Murray (Company Secretary)

Sponsorship

Sponsorship income enables the Traverse to commission and produce new plays and to offer audiences a diverse and exciting programme of events throughout the year.

We would like to thank the following companies for their support:

MAJOR SPONSORS

CORPORATE ASSOCIATE SCHEME

Sunday Herald
Scottish Life the PENSION company
United Distillers & Vintners
Laurence Smith & Son Wine Merchants
Willis Corroon Scotland Ltd
Wired Nomad
Alistir Tait FGA - Antiques & Fine Jewellery
Nicholas Groves Raines - Architects
KPMG
Amanda Howard Associates
Alan Thienot Champagne
Bairds Fine and Country Wines
Communicate
The Wellcome Trust
The Traverse Trivia Quiz in association with Tennants

The Traverse receives financial assistance for its educational and development work from Calouste Gulbenkian Foundation, John Lewis Partnership, Peggy Ramsay Foundation, The Yapp Charitable Trusts, Binks Trust, The Bulldog Prinsep Theatrical Trust, Esmee Fairbairn Trust, Gannochy Trust, Gordon Fraser Charitable Trust, The Garfield Weston Foundation, JSP Pollitzer Charitable Trust, The Hope Trust, The Steel Trust, Paul Hamlyn Foundation, The Craignish Trust, Lindsay's Charitable Trust, Tay Charitable Trust, Ernest Cook Trust, The Education Institute of Scotland, supporting arts projects produced by and for children.

With thanks to:

Navy Blue Design Consultants & Stewarts, graphic designers and printers for the Traverse.
Max Cant for VIS Entertainment plc for Helmet Art Work.
Arts & Business for management and mentoring services.
Purchase of the Traverse Box Office, computer network and technical and training equipment has been made possible with money from The Scottish Arts Council National Lottery Fund.
Douglas and John would like to thank all the actors who took part in *Helmet* workshops.

Traverse Theatre Registered Charity No. SC002368

Paines Plough Registered Charity No. 267523

Contacts

Paines Plough

4th Floor
43 Aldwych
London
WC2B 4DN
Tel: +44 (0) 20 7240 4533
Fax: +44 (0 20 7240 4534
Email: office@painesplough.com
Web site   www.painesplough.com

Traverse Theatre

Cambridge Street
Edinburgh
EH1 2ED
Tel: +44 (0) 131 228 3223
Fax: +44 (0) 131 229 8443
Email: admin@traverse.co.uk
Web Site   www.traverse.co.uk
               www.virtualtraverse.co.uk

First published in 2002 by Oberon Books Ltd.
(incorporating Absolute Classics)
521 Caledonian Road, London N7 9RH
Tel: 020 7607 3637 / Fax: 020 7607 3629

e-mail: oberon.books@btinternet.com

A catalogue record for this book is available from the British
Library.

ISBN: 1 84002 275 2

Cover design: Navy Blue

Cover illustration: Max Cant for VIS Entertainment plc

Printed in Great Britain by Antony Rowe Ltd, Reading.

Author's Note

For anyone interested/brave/drunk enough to stage *Helmet* themselves, please feel free to alter some of the game references in the play. Specifically the new console which Roddy is looking forward to. There's always one on the horizon so please make sure you're up to date, because real Helmets always are. Don't go mad though, a lot of the games are classics and would still be on his conversation list. Have fun.

DM

A million thank yous to everyone from The Performing Arts Lab, especially John Retallack and Bryony Lavery and also to all the inhabitants of Softworld. Without whom…

Characters

SAL

Twenty-five. Sal is an Indian man who has lived
in Scotland all his life. He has an acid tongue,
particularly when it comes to dealing with teenagers
like Roddy who linger in the shop all day. The shop
was his last chance to show his father that he can
be a big success like his brother Junior.

RODDY a.k.a Helmet

Between fourteen and seventeen. Games. Computer
games. That's it. That's all he thinks about. A pale
incoherent boy with an unfortunate haircut. His real
life stinks so he climbs into games to make the time
go quicker. He idolizes Sal. The feeling is *not* mutual.

Instructions

Graphics

You are in 'The Zone', a half empty computer games shop at the very close of day. The till is stage right, a Playstation and N64 set up and running back stage left. A centre shelf is barely covered by empty game boxes. Posters and thumbed magazines everywhere else. There is an exit to the store room behind the counter and an exit into the street stage left.

The Game

There are five levels to the game. Some are two player, some single player. If a character makes a mistake or gets hurt, their energy goes down. Energy can get boosted as they go along. If all their energy disappears they 'die'. If a character 'dies' the scene will start again from the beginning or from the last important plot point. When the play begins each character has three lives.

Power-ups

Extra lives can be picked up by acts of kindness or boosts to the character's energy.

Sound Effects

Sounds will tell you if a player loses energy or a life. After a death the lights snap to black and return to full almost immediately. The scene plays with identical blocking until the problem moment from before. This moment must be dodged for the stage to be completed. In a full production two screens to either side of the stage will show the characters energy bar which fades as their energy goes down. It also displays the number of lives left for each character and any other information needed.

The Story

This is the shop's last day of business. Sal is the owner and is waiting for his wife to return from the bank. One of his regulars, Roddy, turns up instead.

Remember…if you die, the noise will ring out, the lights go down and a life disappears from the screen. The lights return and the scene begins again. Good luck.

LEVEL ONE

Tuesday, 7.05pm

The shop. Empty and tired. SAL is performing last rites. Switching off, shutting up. The screens read 'Level One'. Full energy and lives for both.

SAL: (*To himself.*) Plugs, safe, alarms, shutters, keys. Plugs, safe, alarms, shutters, keys. Plugs, safe, alarms, shutters… keys…keys…where are the keys? Keys? (*Closes his eyes.*) She's taken the keys with her. Brilliant. Oh that is brilliant. So I'm here until she gets back. Brilliant. (*Seeing something.*) Wait a minute, where's all the Diddy Kong gone, man?

> *Enter RODDY at high speed. He bolts past SAL and flees to the TVs at the rear of the stage like a moth to a flame. When it clicks that they're off he freezes. He can't understand it.*

Ho! Out! Helmet go home. Shut. We are shut, the dream is over. Shut! Go back to your miserable life with the real people. Shut!

RODDY: Consoles off?

SAL: The consoles are off and the shop is shut. It's as easy as that.

RODDY: How are they off?

SAL: Just. (*No signs of life.*) Staring at them isn't going to help, Helmet, they're off.

RODDY: See if I bring in…eh…what swap would I get… what's the…

SAL: Helmet! Stop. Deep breaths. Listen. The shop is shut. I'm not going to stand here listening to all these questions. It's pointless. Now please, go home.

Pause. No movement.

Helmet…

RODDY: Can you no put Crazy Taxi on?

SAL: Go home!

Pause. RODDY dives for the controller of the Playstation, SAL flakes and grabs him. He has to pull his legs to get him away from the console. There's shouts from both. SAL is furious. He physically shoves RODDY to the door.

This is all your fault! You never know when to shut up, Helmet. You never know when to listen to people. Now get out. *Get out!*

He gives RODDY a further push to get out the door. RODDY dies. Death noise, blackout, life lost on screen.

7.05pm

The shop. Empty and tired. SAL is performing last rites. Switching off, shutting up. The screens read 'Level One'. RODDY is now on two lives.

SAL: (*To himself.*) Plugs, safe, alarms, shutters, keys. Plugs, safe, alarms, shutters, keys. Plugs, safe, alarms, shutters… keys…keys…where are the keys? Keys? (*Closes his eyes.*) She's taken the keys with her. Brilliant. Oh that is brilliant. So I'm here until she gets back. Brilliant. (*Seeing something.*) Wait a minute, where's all the Diddy Kong gone, man?

Enter RODDY at high speed. He bolts past SAL and flees to the TVs at the rear of the stage like a moth to a flame. When it clicks that they're off he freezes. He can't understand it.

Ho! Out! Helmet go home. Shut. We are shut, the dream is over. Shut! Go back to your miserable life with the real people. Shut!

RODDY: Consoles off?

SAL: The consoles are off and the shop is shut. It's as easy as that.

RODDY: How are they off?

SAL: Just. (*No signs of life.*) Staring at them isn't going to help, Helmet, they're off.

RODDY: See if I bring in...eh...what swap would I get... what's the...

SAL: Helmet! Stop. Deep breaths. Listen. The shop is shut. I'm not going to stand here listening to all these questions. It's pointless. Now please, go home.

RODDY: I promise I'll be quiet if you let me stay. Please Sal.

SAL: Oh for...

RODDY: I'll no say anything, I'll just stand. No questions.

SAL: No man, shut innit.

RODDY: Is Virtual Headlice in? It's out tomorrow. Is it in?

SAL: Are you touched? I've told you a million times that the shop is shutting tomorrow. Forever. I told you two hours ago. You'll have to linger somewhere else. Now go on.

RODDY's energy goes down.

RODDY: What was the best driving game on the N64?

SAL: Unbelievable. No-one listens to a word I...

RODDY: Was it Cruising World? Or F1? I like Top Gear Rally but it's ancient. Virtual Headlice is going to be ace man! Is it in? It's out tomorrow? I've got money.

SAL: The shop is shutting. My shop is closing down. There's a sign in the window, I've told you every single day for a month, what else do you need? Do you want me to whisper it to you while you sleep? Do you want a tattoo? Go home!

RODDY loses more energy.

RODDY: Where's Bindi?

SAL: Eh?

RODDY: Where's Bindi? Isnae she the one that usually does the shutters and that? Where is she?

SAL: She's at the bank if you must know.

RODDY: At seven at night?

SAL: She's at the bank.

RODDY: Banks are shut man. What's the best Platinum game? It's Metal Gear Solid innit?

SAL: The whereabouts of my wife is none of your business. She's at the bank. Where else would she be? She has nowhere else to… (*Reminded of something awful.*) Damn.

Death noise, blackout, SAL loses a life on screen.

Lights up.

7.11pm

RODDY: Where's Bindi?

SAL: Eh?

RODDY: Where's Bindi? Isnae she the one that usually does the shutters and that? Where is she?

SAL: She's at the bank if you must know.

RODDY: At seven at night?

SAL: She's at the bank.

RODDY: Banks are shut man. What's the best Platinum game? It's Metal Gear Solid innit?

SAL: She... I'm not thinking about that now. I've got more important things to think about. (*Turning angrily on RODDY.*) Like where have all my Diddy Kong Racing gone?

RODDY: Eh?

SAL: There were three boxes of Diddy Kong here and now they're gone. Gone are the Diddy Kong and I want names.

RODDY: Eh?

SAL: Your pals. The wee casuals. Ned boys. They steal empty boxes, I know they do.

RODDY: They're no pals, man, I hate them.

SAL: What can you do with the boxes anyway? They're empty! You can't live in them, you can't marry them and I'm pretty sure you can't eat them. They must wear them. In fact I'll bet that somewhere up in hell hole land a Diddy Kong Racing hat is a symbol of authority.

RODDY: (*Not laughing.*) You're such a laugh man.

SAL: (...) Out.

RODDY: I thought this was your dad's shop.

SAL: Out.

RODDY: Is it your fault the shop's shutting? Is it? Is it your fault the shop's shutting? Sal?

SAL turns away and dies. Death noise, blackout, life less on the screen.

7.12pm

RODDY: (*Not laughing.*) You're such a laugh, man.

SAL: (…) Out.

RODDY: I thought this was your dad's shop.

SAL: Out.

RODDY: Is it your fault the shop's shutting?

SAL decides to shrug this off as a joke.

SAL: Well according to the old boy I'm to blame for everything that goes wrong in the world so it must be my fault. Traffic congestion, *Who Wants To Be A Millionaire?*, Chickenpox, they're all down to me in his eyes, so this is no different. No, Roddy the Helmet, it is not my fault the shop is shutting. It is your fault. You and all the other pale wee dopes who hover in here all day and night scaring away the real customers.

RODDY: Sal, you know how you said that when I'm thirty I can get a job in here…

SAL: Unbelievable.

RODDY: Will I get to test the games out that folk bring in for swaps.

SAL: (…) Yes.

RODDY: Yeeeees!!!!!

Power-up noise, energy up on RODDY's screen.

Gonna put the Playstation Two on?

SAL: No. It's quarter past seven.

RODDY: Ah but you said two people have to be here to shut the shop and Bindi's not here and I am so I can be the other person that shuts the shop because it'll be two

26

people and it'll be me and I'm here. Gonna put the Playstation Two on?

SAL: You'll just hang about like always asking daft questions.

RODDY: I won't. If you put the Playstation Two on I promise I'll go straight away.

SAL: So if I don't you'll stay?

RODDY: Aye.

SAL: (*Confused.*) What?

RODDY: It's a deal. Put Quake Three on, no Star Wars Starfighter, no Fifa… WWF… No put on…eh… Crazy Taxi.

SAL: No! Shut up.

RODDY: Put on the Playstation One then.

SAL: It's… I… How… (*Relenting just to shut him up.*) Oh alright. Thirty seconds though. Thirty seconds then out.

RODDY: Yeeeeessss!!!!!

RODDY gains back an extra life. Power-up noise and a heart back on the screen.

SAL: Driver's in there, you can play that. Thirty seconds. I'm making a phonecall so stay quiet. No questions.

RODDY: What about questions about things that aren't about games? Like houses? Or dogs? What about questions about dogs? Or Catholics?

SAL: Play!

SAL switches on the Playstation and even as it loads RODDY is gone. He just drops out of real life, gripping onto the controller like a float in a swimming pool. SAL goes over to the counter, picks up the phone and dials. The phone is a large phone/fax machine with a wee screen to show numbers and information. He's phoning his brother Junior.

(*The following speech is in Punjabi.*) Hello Junior? Is that Junior? Is this the Indian Sun restaurant? I'm afraid I have a complaint. My wife and I had a meal there three years ago, but now she's dead. I think it was your food that killed her, you know what I mean? I want my money back. (*He's been rumbled.*) Ha ha ha (*English.*) Junior man what's up? Yeah man yeah. The shop innit. (*Punjabi.*) Listen man is my missus there? Bindi, is she there? I dunno, just thought she might be there. The Clydesdale. No, she's got the keys. Yeah, will if you do. Oh don't start, it's not my fault she took the…oh shut up. Nothing's going to happen. Okay, okay, just don't tell Dad, right. I will! Tonight. I'll tell him. Yeah, bye.

RODDY: (*Not looking away from the screen throughout this.*) Who was that?

SAL: It was God, you've to go home.

RODDY: Was it your brother?

SAL: …

RODDY: He's got an ace car your brother. It's like something from Gran Turismo Two. Miles better than your car. Bindi was talking about him the other day. Says he's rich and he's got a big house, but you have to stay with your mum and dad even though you're married.

Something happens in the game he's playing.

Ooooh no way man! Was she there?

SAL loses energy with all the sounds that entails.

Know how you said if I really wanted Virtual Headlice I should go out and get it on my own? You know, use my inivitive and that…

SAL: (*Long suffering.*) Aye. You don't get anything for nothing. You get exactly what you put in. It's all about effort. Effort and concentration. Two things you know nothing about. All this crap sucks it out of you. You're all a bunch of dim, slow-witted ghosts with no will power. You're going to end up as nothing and it'll be the games' fault. And keep your nose out of my business, right! Get out. Get out!

RODDY dies. Death noise, less a heart on screen.

Lights up.

7.25pm

RODDY: Who was that?

SAL: It was God. You've to go home.

RODDY: (*Turns away from the screen and looks adoringly at SAL.*) I love playing games, man.

SAL gives RODDY a long hard look of disgust as the lights go down to blackout.

End of Level One.

LEVEL TWO

8.15pm

Screen now reads 'Level Two'. The Playstation has been left running. RODDY stands facing SAL, who sits on the counter absently flicking through a magazine. RODDY has a look of total admiration on his face.

SAL: (*Without looking up.*) Stop it.

RODDY: Stop what?

SAL: Stop staring at me. It's pathetic and I know you're doing it.

RODDY: I'm not.

SAL: You are.

RODDY: See in school right. I had to do this thing about the person you most thingby. The person you most admire. Guess who I done? Guess.

SAL: Super Mario.

RODDY: Yeah I did him first, but it turns out he's no real. But is that right? 'Cause he might be, you don't really know. Mrs Grey says she does know. He's great, Super Mario. He's Super. 'Cause he's a plumber right, but he also saves Princesses and that.

SAL: Just try getting him out on a Sunday though. He's not so super then.

RODDY: So after Mario I did you.

Pause. SAL gives RODDY a very worried look and then returns to his magazine.

SAL: That's one of the saddest things I've ever heard man.

RODDY: 'Cause you own a games shop, you know all about games and you're always saying stuff I don't hear properly so you must be totally clever. If I could be anyone I'd be you.

SAL: I take it all back. *That* is the saddest thing I've ever heard. Helmet, let me assure you, with absolute conviction, that being me is not the game you think it is. It's bleedin' awful, truth be told.

RODDY: How?

Pause, no answer.

Who's yours?

SAL: Who's my what?

RODDY: Who's the guy you most admire? And you can't say Mario, he's already been picked.

SAL: (*Sarcastically.*) That's a blow. (*Thinking.*) Who I most admire? Jerry Seinfeld.

RODDY: Oh aye, he's ace.

SAL: You don't know who that is.

RODDY: I do.

SAL: No you don't.

RODDY: Aye I do.

SAL: You don't. You think you do but you don't.

RODDY: I do! Look.

RODDY goes off to the shelves on a search for something. He's not listening to SAL.

SAL: Two million an episode. And it's finished now. He never needs to work again. He just sits in the house being hilarious and making money. That's what I should

31

have done, stand up comedy. Just standing there, alone, just you and the mic and the audience. No-one can tell you what to do once you're up doing your act. And I bet I could do it, given the right audience. Folk are forever saying I'm funny. Make a change from what I'm doing now. Stand up bloody tragedy. Right, Helmet?

RODDY: (*Oblivious.*) Eh?

SAL: Exactly. I did it once. Well, nearly. I signed up to this competition in the student union. But… It wasn't to be. It was a difficult audience. It was a *very* difficult audience. So…oh well. (*Snaps out of it.*) It's decided then, right Helmet, from now on I'm a multi-milionaire stand up comedian. I'll tell Dad the happy news tonight. 'Dad, I've bankrupted the shop and ruined your life, but fear not, I'm going into comedy!' That'll get a laugh at least.

RODDY has found what he's been looking for. A game box. He hands it to SAL.

What?

RODDY: Read the back.

SAL: (*Reading.*) 'Battle against time as the Nimrod virus sweeps the globe turning innocent millions into blood sucking Vampires. You play cunning FBI agent… Gerry Seinfeld, who has only three days to save the world'. No way.

RODDY: See.

SAL: Yeah, but…

RODDY: So anyway if I could be anyone I'd be you.

SAL: Oh for…you don't even know me. You just stand in my shop all day asking thick questions.

RODDY: (*Slowly.*) To truly know a character one must not only observe his environment but also how he reacts to that environment and the characters within it. His progress into or from that environment tells you everything you need to know about said character's journey through existence.

A big 'What the…?!' look from SAL. Pause.

It's from the instructions to Deathtime Bonanza Two. That's my favourite book.

SAL: Helmet, the instructions to Deathtime Bonanza Two are not a book. They are instructions.

RODDY: It's got a good story.

SAL: It's not a story, it's a game, innit. There's a difference. Games aren't stories and stories aren't games.

RODDY: Sal can I stay until Bindi gets back? I promise I won't do anything.

SAL thinks for a minute. He's secretly enjoying this little burst of admiration, so…

SAL: Oh…okay.

RODDY: Yeeeeesss!!!!

All RODDY's lives return and he's boosted to full energy. Lots of power-up noises. SAL smiles despite himself at having the ability to make someone as happy as this. He gets an extra life for his trouble complete with sound effects.

SAL: Calm down, she'll be here any minute.

RODDY: Thanks Sal. Thanks man. I promise I'll no do anything. I'll just stand.

SAL: I don't mind you playing the games or anything, just don't ask loads of questions.

RODDY: Right. No questions. Right.

SAL goes back to his reading. A slight pause for RODDY to control himself but the dam bursts and out comes...

What's your favourite N64 game where do games go that don't sell do they still make Dreamcasts how do you get all the crystals in Crash Three is Actua Soccer Two better than Actua one what's a Gameboy Advance if I had Tunnel B1 what could I swap it with what gun do you use for Time Crisis how come the shop's shutting?

Completely ignored by SAL. RODDY dies. Blackout, loss of life.

8.21pm

SAL: I don't mind you playing the games or anything. Just don't ask loads of questions.

RODDY: Right. No questions. Right.

SAL goes back to his reading. A longer pause now as RODDY holds back the flood with slightly more success. But it can't last...

What came first the megadrive or the SNES where do steering wheels plug in does a Playstation work on computer monitor why do Japanese games come out before British games if I had Driver Two what could I swap it with when's the Gamecube coming out how come the shop's shutting?

Again, completely ignored by SAL. RODDY dies, blackout, less a life on screen.

8.21pm

SAL: I don't mind you playing games or anything. Just don't ask loads of questions.

RODDY: Right. No questions. Right.

This is a real test for RODDY. No lives left. He wanders, he fidgets, he claps his hands to his mouth like a man about to be sick. SAL goes to the phone and tries to phone Junior again. It's engaged. He sees RODDY struggling with himself.

SAL: What's up with you?

RODDY: (*Still covering his mouth.*) Mumfet.

SAL: Stop doing that.

RODDY: I'm not asking questions.

SAL: I am. 'Where's my stupid wife?' being the first. 'What the hell will I tell my dad tonight about the shop?' close at number two. And number three, 'Where did I go wrong?' He's going to kill me, man. I'm the first one out of the whole lot of us to fail at something. Concentration and effort. Yeah right.

RODDY: It's not your fault, man. It's that Electronic Boutique. You could never win. They've got carpets and everything.

Power-up noise and new life for SAL as he dodges taking the blame for the business.

SAL: Ah ha! Thank you Helmet, exactly. I couldnae believe it when they opened up. It's not my fault. I couldn't compete. Not even my dad could make this place work. And now Bindi's not speaking to me. 'Junior's got a house. Junior's making a success of his business, Junior stuck to what he knows, Junior can fly.' And now she's gone and we all know where to.

RODDY: (*Matter of fact.*) To the bank. Talking about banks…

SAL: And to make matters worse, the final straw that's nailed the coffin to the camel's back, is that when my own wife is out *there*…wherever, I seem to be spending the night with an ugly, stupid wee retard whose brain has turned to mush with all the crap I sell him.

Pause. For some reason this has broken through and RODDY is hurt. Energy goes down badly, but he's not dead. He turns to go but only gets to the door. Stops. There's nothing good out there. He doubles back to the Playstation. Grips the controller, gets into the game, feels better. Feels nothing.

Helmet. Helmet I'm sorry. I didn't mean you. I'm just sad because the shop's shutting. Helmet can you hear me? Stop playing that a minute. I'm saying sorry. Stop playing…

Tries to take the controller away from RODDY, but he has an iron first clamped round it. Eyes fixed on the screen.

Helmet, let go of the controller. Look at me. Helmet. For… Helmet.

RODDY: *My name's not Helmet it's Roddy. It's Roddy. I'm not ugly.*

A battle cry from Street fighter complete with move.

SONIC BOOOOOOOOOOOOMMMM!!!!!!!!!

SAL is killed. Blackout, death noise, loss of heart.

8.25pm

SAL: Ah ha! Thank you Helmet, exactly. I couldnae believe it when they opened up. It's not my fault. I couldn't compete. Not even my dad could make this place work. And now Bindi's not speaking to me. 'Junior's got a house. Junior's making a success of his business, Junior stuck to what he knows, Junior can fly.' And now she's gone and we all know where to.

RODDY: (*Matter of fact.*) To the bank. Talking about banks, I've got the money for Virtual Headlice.

RODDY dumps two bank bags of change on the counter.

It's going to be ace, man. Like Micromachines except you drive wee lice around folks' heads and there's a secret level where you drive up folks' bums! Ha ha ha ha. Ace. There it is forty three pounds.

SAL: Where'd you get this? Did you steal it?

RODDY: No man, I found it. Earned it I mean. My dad gave me it.

SAL: (*Not entirely satisfied.*) Mmmm.

RODDY: So can I get the game?

SAL: It's not out, it's been delayed.

RODDY: *What????*

Loss of energy for RODDY with noises.

Blackout.

End of Level Two.

LEVEL THREE

8.45pm

SAL sits on the desk again. RODDY is in the middle of the shop, holding a cracked and empty Playstation game case in one hand and a game box from the shelf in the other. He holds them high above his head. The consoles are off. Screen reads 'Level Three'.

RODDY: This?

SAL: No.

RODDY: (*Picks up another game case.*) This?

SAL: No.

RODDY: Ehmm… (*He picks up another case.*) This?

SAL: *No!* Look, Helmet, I can't help but feel we've been over this before, but you've obviously failed to grasp the finer details. Let me explain…you see, what you have in your right hand is an empty, cracked Playstation game case which you've picked up from a puddle. In your left hand is a brand new game worth forty pounds. You can't swap them. Repeat: you cannot swap them.

RODDY: (*Looking round.*) What about…?

SAL: No! Listen! No swaps! You've got forty odd pounds in those bags, why don't you just buy a new game? You can have the pleasure of being The Zone's last customer. (*Under his breath.*) Double our bloody takings for the day.

RODDY: I'm saving that money for Virtual Headlice but.

SAL: It's delayed, innit. It might not come out anyway. I was reading it's having trouble getting a certificate.

RODDY: Is it an eighteen? If it's an eighteen will you sell me it?

SAL: Well *I* won't because the shop's shutting, but no doubt
someone will.

RODDY: (*Remembering.*) Oh yeah, the shop's shutting.

RODDY's energy goes down a little.

SAL: No-one pays any attention to the age things on
the back of the games anyway. They should though.
I wouldn't have some of that stuff in my house. 'Member
Goldeneye? I couldn't believe it! You shoot a guy and he
flaps down into a pool of blood. And you're doing it,
pushing the buttons. And that was just the start, GTA
Three, Carmegedon, Rayman, you name it.

RODDY: Rayman!

SAL: And you're *always* waiting for something new to
come out. Something better. The best stuff's always on
the way. Better graphics, better gameplay, better sound,
it's a total con. Even the machines; first it was the
Dreamcast that was going to send sales through the roof,
then it's the Playstation Two, then the Xbox. But nothing
ever happens. Nothing changes. Just an underwhelming
anti-climax followed by a million questions about when
the next one's coming out. It's only after you've been
bombarded with all the new and improved stuff you look
back and think 'actually the SNES wasn't too bad. At
least it had decent games.' If it's a good game, why do
you need all the graphics and sound and that. You'd
think folk would be happy with a good, solid, reliable
game they could play. Why do people always need
something new and flashier? No-one's ever happy with
what they've got.

RODDY: I am. When's the Gamecube coming out?

SAL: You see that's…

RODDY: Were you joking about Rayman? 'Cos he hasn't got any thingby in his games. Violence.

SAL: What?

RODDY: An' I was thinking about it anyroads, the other day. Em…see how old folk say, like, the younger generation and violence and that? And how it's 'cause of games? Well…how come they had a war? Didn't they? The old folk? They had two, Mrs Grey says. But *they* never had a Playstation Two. Or a Playstation One. Or an Dreamcast. Or even a Megadrive. But they still had a war. Killing hundreds of folk. Millions of dead folk. And like (*Struggling.*) eh…so…you can't say games make people want to kill people. It was *not* having a Playstation. They couldn't think of anything else to do so they had a war. How far can you get in Banjo Kazooi?

SAL: (…) You lost me a bit at the end there, Roddy, but that was very nearly conversation. Nice one. (*To the door.*) Where is she? Do you think she's alright? I mean it's quarter to nine.

RODDY: Thought you said she was with your big brother?

SAL's energy goes down a little.

SAL: He's not my big brother. He's my wee brother.

RODDY: How come you hate your wee brother? I think he's ace.

SAL: You don't even know my wee brother!

RODDY: Aye but he sounds ace. He really *listens* to you.

SAL: (*Stunned/bewildered.*) He really…*eh?*

RODDY: And he's got no issues or that. He just gets on with it. No complaints. And he's got an ace car. I've seen his car. It's like something from Gran Turismo Two.

SAL's energy goes down some more.

SAL: (*Very nearly furious.*) Listen, I'd have no complaints either if I was him. He got *given* that restaurant by the way. It's not really his, it's his wife's. Things just fall into his lap. And all that caring sharing rubbish, that's new! He never used to be like that. Underneath he's still a sneaky wee get. He used to totally hate it when Dad let me work in the shop, so he's like that 'Sal's nicking fireworks' and from then on in I'm in the store emptying deliveries. It was his idea to nick the bloody fireworks! I did it for him. But ever since the money's come in he's all, 'Keep your chin up mate, it'll happen'. And all this 'it might help if you spend some time in the restaurant, soak up business techniques, success breeds success'. I'll tell you what breeds success, a rich father in law.

RODDY: (*Very uncomfortable.*) Do you think the Gamecube will have DVD?

SAL: And guess who's idea this (*The shop.*) was? He's like, 'You've tried University and that didn't work, you've tried comedy and that didn't work, you've tried restaurants and that didn't work, it's time to take a risk. Computer games! That's where the money is.' But now, surprise surprise, he's joining in with the old boy, 'You should've stuck to what you know.' No issues! I don't have any issues. He's the one with the issues. And of course we've usually got two sets of keys don't we, but I had to hand one set to the estate agent yesterday. I can't leave the shop open and I don't want to phone home in case Junior's grassed me in to Dad about us shutting.

RODDY: Are you going to open another games shop?

SAL: Pffft! Yeah right. If I don't see another Playstation for as long as I live it'll be too soon. Stick to what you know. I'll probably have to go and work in Junior's restaurant. Or maybe I should be like Sega and give up on the whole thing. Sometimes it's better to just admit defeat. Cut your losses. No matter how good your games are, there's always a Sony or a Microsoft out there who'll swallow you up. For every SNES there's a Megadrive, for every Saturn there's a Playstation, for every Gamegear there's a Gameboy, for every me there's a Junior, for every you there's a …well…whatever. You know what I mean.

SAL lets out a heartfelt sigh. Pause. Both energies go down. Is this the end? RODDY can't let that happen. He pulls a shared memory out the bag.

RODDY: Here, remember that time when this guy was playing the N64 and it was dead busy and all of sudden he started breakdancing?

SAL: No.

RODDY: You must, man. It was Saturday, it was dead busy. He was old, he was a proper guy. He'd been playing… what was it… Killer Instinct. This song came on and he jumps back like that, whoosh, and started doing all these moves on the floor. It was ace, man. He was spinning and popping and then you joined in and like, grabbed him and this thing came flying out! That was amazing, man! That's one of the best things I've ever seen, that guy breakdancing.

Pause.

SAL: (*Slowly.*) Helmet…he wasn't breakdancing. That guy was choking to death.

RODDY: Eh?

SAL: He was choking to death! He had a bit of pie lodged in his throat. I grabbed him and forced it loose by shoogling up and down. The pie came flying out and hit Bindi in the face for God's sake!

RODDY: So he wasn't breakdancing?

SAL: No.

RODDY: He was choking?

SAL: Yes.

RODDY: Aw right. But I was clapping along with the music!

A slight pause. SAL starts to laugh. Just a wee bit at first, but it soon escalates into the laughter that comes hand in hand with desperate situations.

What? What is it? What is it?

RODDY starts to laugh by proxy. Soon the pair of them are laughing uproariously. RODDY is delighted to have said something that makes Sal so happy, even if he doesn't know what it is. He returns to full lives and energy. SAL is glad to be laughing at all. It's been a long time. He gets a boost of energy and an extra life. RODDY feels that he's on a roll and shouts through tears of laughter.

I'll tell you something else really funny man…

SAL: (*Through laughs.*) What?

RODDY: Know how I've been waiting for Virtual Headlice for ages…?

SAL: You asked me every day, on the hour, every hour, ha ha ha.

RODDY: Know how you said I should work out how to get the money and use my imagination and concentrate…

SAL: What was I thinking? Imagination…

RODDY: (*As if telling the punchline to the world's funniest joke.*) Well tonight I went and punched a woman and stole her bag and the bag had forty pounds in it!!!!! Ha ha ha ha ha!!!!!

SAL: Ha ha h… (*Suddenly realising. He freezes mid laugh. He turns and looks at the hysterical RODDY.*) What?

RODDY: It was in Orange Arch. I was really scared, right, I wasnae gonna do it. But I bombed it up behind her, boosh! Down she goes. I grabbed the bag and bombed it. Forty quid!! Ha ha ha!

SAL is now completely stone-faced. He watches RODDY cope with laughter with cold fury. RODDY notices that SAL isn't laughing and slips through the gears of happiness back to a teary-eyed sobriety.

What? You're not laughing.

Pause.

What?

Pause.

Why aren't you laughing?

SAL: Because it's not funny. *It's not funny!* (*Punjabi.*) How dare you? You attacked a woman to buy a game? (*English.*) How dare you come here and say that I told you to do it? What's wrong with you? Have you lost your mind? And to treat it as a joke and tell it as a story?

RODDY: (*Beginning to panic. He wasn't expecting this.*) You were laughing at that guy choking.

SAL: That's completely different man. (*Punjabi.*) What am I going to do? What am I going to do? Oh no. (*English.*) Phone the police.

RODDY: No Sal. Sal. Don't. I had to get the game. I thought it came out the day.

SAL: I'm going to phone the police.

RODDY: It's not true. I made the story up so you'd like me better and think I was tough and could come up with ideas like you.

SAL: Yeah right.

RODDY: I did. It's not even true. I promise.

SAL: Where'd you get it then? Eh?

RODDY: It's my dad's bookies money. He keeps it in a jar by his bed. I counted it out.

SAL: Liar! I know you're lying because you don't have the imagination to come up with a story like that.

RODDY: (*Nearly crying.*) I just thought you'd like it. It was so you'd like me.

SAL: Helmet I'm going to say one thing to you and I want you to listen very, very carefully. If you've never understood anything else I've ever said, understand this. I've never liked you. I've…never…liked…*you.* And no matter what you or any of the other idiots that come in here think, we are not the same. We don't live on the same planet. In a language that you'd understand, I'm a Playstation and you're an N64. Okay we're in the same shop, but we play different games. Know what I mean? You stay here. (*Dials.*) Hello Police…yeah…

RODDY turns away frozen. A pause…then… RODDY dies, blackout, death noise, loss of life on screen.

8.50pm

From blackout straight into huge laughs. RODDY is delighted to have said something that makes SAL so happy, even if he doesn't know what it is.

RODDY: I tell you something else really funny.

SAL: (*Through laughs.*) What?

RODDY: Know how I've been waiting for Virtual Headlice for ages…?

SAL: You asked me every day, on the hour, every hour, ha ha ha.

RODDY: Know how you said I should work out for myself how to get the money and use my imagination…

SAL: What was I thinking? Imagination…

RODDY: Well I…eh..oh…forget it.

SAL: Oh God. What would I do without you. Probably go out of business, oh no wait.

SAL's laughter is running out. There is small, happy pause. RODDY is struggling to follow his comedy success with another story that will make SAL like him.

RODDY: My wee brother Charlie died in a fire when he was only one.

Blackout.

End of Level Three.

LEVEL FOUR

Screen reads 'Level Four'. This level is different. RODDY stands facing the audience.

RODDY: My wee brother Charlie died in a fire when he was only one.

It was thirteen days after my mum had gone. She left a note. She said good-bye to me but not my dad. She cried over Charlie's pram, then ran out the door without her coat on. She must have been cold.

My big brother Philip is in the army.

He came home when Dad got into trouble with the police for being sad. Philip's friend told him that mum was in Girvan. Girvan has a beach and puggies and nothing else.

Dad took me and Charlie to Girvan in the car.

I had more room on the way back, but it took much longer.

We had a caravan on a hill and it smelt of pish. Me and Charlie stayed in the puggies when Dad was looking for Mum.

I played Sega Rally, Virtua Fighter, Star Wars Trilogy, Sensible Soccer, a flying game on a bike and House of the Dead with the gun. I said to Charlie that the arcade version is much better than the Saturn version. But he didn't know what I was talking about. He was only one.

On the second night Dad didn't come back. The woman from the caravan park told us that he'd phoned to say he'd be late. I was to give Charlie his dinner. But he didn't want that dinner. So I made chips.

After dinner I went to play Virtua Fighter in the puggies down at the harbour. I got to the second last level. A guy said 'You're really good at that game, wee man.' You're really good at that game, wee man.

When I got back the caravan was on fire and Charlie was in it.

The screens go off.

I saw…

I saw….

I tried to drive the car to get Dad. But I couldn't do it. There were firemen and policemen and strangers but no-one could get Charlie out. He died in a fire and he was only one.

It was funny because Mum and Dad were there. But not in a nice way.

Dad never really spoke to Charlie, but he still tried to go into the fire to get him out.

I was in the car. I sat in the car and thought about Gran Turismo.

The screens slowly fade in again.

There's two hundred and fifty cars in Gran Turismo and full motion video replays. You have to get different licences and it's dead hard to get the A licence. There are no cheats available.

When I got home I had to see a counsellor. He let me play games in his office, but he never played. Except once and he couldn't do it. He didn't even know how to hold the controller. It's sad. But mostly he just wrote things down.

My brother Philip was crying on the phone. But not as much as Mum. He doesn't come back. Mum does. But not in a nice way.

I don't have a Playstation anymore. I don't have an N64.
I don't have a megadrive. No SNES. No Gameboy. I don't
have a Saturn or a Dreamcast.

I asked for a Playstation Two for my Christmas. But
I didn't get it. I still buy the games though. I keep them
in a box under my bed. Just in case.

Sometimes when you have no lives left, you play better.
Because you know that if you make a mistake you die.
You think faster and do things you didn't know you
could do.

That's why I don't like those cheats that give you infinite
lives. You don't get the feeling that you might die.
Sometimes that's good. And sometimes it's bad.

But sometimes…sometimes the computer just decides
to win. It just decides that you are going to die and it's
not fair.

And there's nothing you can do about it.

You can be playing really well and not hurting anyone.
Just lying there sleeping. And the game finishes.

All your lives are gone at once.

It's not fair.

And there's nothing you can do about it.

Blackout.

End of Level Four.

LEVEL FIVE

8.53pm

Screen reads 'Level Five'. They don't speak for a moment.

SAL: I didn't know that.

RODDY: What?

SAL: That. I didn't know that.

RODDY: What?

SAL: (*Trying not to get angry.*) I didn't know your brother died in a fire.

RODDY: Aye I know. When will the Gamecube be out?

SAL: (…) Roddy…do your mum and dad know that you spend so much time in the shop?

RODDY: (*Shrugs.*) They know I like games. They don't really ask me stuff. And I don't ask them stuff. I like it here 'cause it's like a wee place you can go, do you know what I mean. It's a wee place you can go and no-body can get you. That's why I like games as well. One minute it's four o'clock, next minute it's night time. It makes the time go quicker. What did you say about the Gamecube?

SAL: You know when I throw you out the shop…?

RODDY: It's funny, isn't it? I know you're only joking.

SAL: Well… I did want you out of the shop. I wasn't really joking about that. That's not what I mean. I mean, it's not because I don't like you or anything. You should be out there running about playing football or something.

RODDY: I don't like football.

SAL: It doesn't have to be football, it could be anything.

RODDY: Like what?

SAL: I don't know, anything. What's your favourite sport?

RODDY: I like PGA 97.

SAL: That's a game. That's a golfing game for the Playstation. It's not a sport.

RODDY: Golf's a sport.

SAL: Golf's a sport yes, but golf on the Playstation is not.

RODDY: I don't understand this.

SAL: It's easy!

RODDY: So you want me to play golf?

SAL: *No!* Sorry. No, Roddy. I just want you to get some air. Get some exercise. Or a hobby or something. What do you like at school? What's your favourite thing?

RODDY: I like it when we clean out the cupboards. It's an ace laugh, man, cleaning out cupboards. Ha ha ha.

SAL: Sounds it.

RODDY: This is my favourite thing. Sometimes I think about what it would be like if I was in charge of the shop. I think about it all the time. Daft.

SAL: No man it's not daft. You can do whatever you want. My old man, right, came over from India with nothing. He had no relatives here or nothing. He could hardly speak a word of English and now look at him. He always says all you need in business is effort and concentration. Put the work in and don't get distracted by other things, you know what I mean. If you're distracted you make mistakes.

Pause.

Mind you that's easy for him to say.

RODDY: The Gamecube is going to make everything better. It'll save the day.

SAL: It won't save my day. I hope he doesn't blame Bindi. He thinks everything's her fault. It's no-ones fault. Electronic Boutique and everything.

RODDY: It's going to have a hundred and twenty-five million poloygons per second, textures, lighting, and you can upgrade it.

SAL: I know exactly what he'll say. Effort and bloody concentration. 'When I came here from India…' blah blah blah, if I hear that one more time. It's only a crappy computer games shop!

RODDY: I can't wait for it.

SAL: I'm talented and funny. Folk say I'm talented. I could be a comedian.

RODDY: I cannot wait for Gamecube.

SAL: It was a difficult audience.

RODDY: Sal?

SAL: What?

RODDY: I'm going to open a shop!

SAL: Why not?

RODDY's energy goes up.

RODDY: (*Prompting him.*) With effort and…

SAL: Yeah that's it. Effort and concentration.

RODDY: That's it. That's all you need. I'll be alright. And I'm ace at concentrating. See sometimes when I'm playing a game, my dad'll be shouting me and I'll no hear him. Sal?

SAL: Mmm?

RODDY: Do you think we'll be alright?

SAL: (…) Yes.

> *RODDY's energy goes up some more. But SAL doesn't believe it to be true. He doesn't think RODDY will be okay. His energy goes down and he dies. Blackout, death noise, loss of heart on screen.*

9.05pm

RODDY: Sal?

SAL: What?

RODDY: I'm going to open a shop!

SAL: Why not?

> *RODDY's energy goes up.*

RODDY: (*Prompting him.*) With effort and…

SAL: Yeah that's it. Effort and concentration.

RODDY: That's it. That's all you need. I'll be alright. And I'm ace at concentrating. See sometimes when I'm playing a game, my dad'll be shouting me and I'll no hear him. Sal?

SAL: Mmm?

RODDY: Do you think we'll be alright?

> *SAL goes to speak but can't bring himself to say no. He shrugs and can't look RODDY in the eye.*

Sal? Sal? Do you think we'll be alright? No?

> *RODDY dies, blackout, loss of life on screen.*

9.05pm

RODDY: Sal?

SAL: What?

RODDY: I'm going to open a shop!

SAL: Why not?

RODDY: (*Prompting him.*) With effort and…

SAL: Yeah that's it. Effort and concentration.

RODDY: That's it. That's all you need. I'll be alright. And I'm ace at concentrating. See sometimes when I'm playing a game, my dad'll be shouting me and I'll no hear him. Sal?

SAL: Mmm?

RODDY: Do you think we'll be alright?

SAL: I dunno, maybe. You'll need to get away from games all the time. You won't be able to stay in your room forever.

RODDY: I know.

SAL: You can't just hide away from the real world all the time.

RODDY: I know.

Pause.

SAL: (*Second thoughts.*) No, that's a load of crap, you do what you bloody want. The real world's rubbish, Helmet. If you want to stay in your room, you stay in your room. I've seen the real world and I give you my word – it's not worth seeing. The real world is vile and horrible and boring and fatally depressing. You just play games and don't let anyone tell you it's wrong. It's not wrong. It's right. That's my problem, that's *always* been my problem, I actually pay attention to those idiots that bang on about money and jobs and relationships and responsibility. Effort and concentration! What have they got to do with anything? You see I'm just like you, Helmet, the real world's a bloody mystery half the time, so I prefer thinking about all the other stuff. Like this thing with Junior and Bindi right? I'm sitting here *imagining* all kinds of stuff, *enjoying* my own misery, rather than just facing the boring fact that she prefers sitting in a busy restaurant surrounded by happy folk to sitting in here with me staring into space. It's all in my head, and it always has been. They're not having an affair, they don't have the imagination. But I do. And there's nothing wrong with that. So bugger it. As long as we're in here the real world can piss off. (*Shouts a Punjabi insult to the real world outside the gates, then laughs.*) They'll have to drag us out kicking and screaming. In fact do you know what we're going to do Roddy, my wee brother in arms? We're going to play a game!

RODDY: What, really?

SAL: Why not? We're here for the rest of our lives after all.

RODDY: We can play a two player game.

SAL: Okay. Tekken Three? They're all going back to Interactive tomorrow anyway.

RODDY: What, really? Me against you? No way man. Thanks, Sal. Thanks, man.

SAL: It's in the back. Don't let our enemies break through those shutters.

All RODDY's lives return with all the traditional noises. SAL exits to fetch the game.

RODDY: Thanks man. I hired it once from the video shop. I've never even seen you play a game! Me against you.

SAL: (*Off.*) Don't get too excited, I'll have you beaten in two seconds.

The phone rings.

RODDY: Ha ha ha. Sal, see if you open another shop, can I work there when I'm thirty?

SAL: (*Off.*) Yes. Get the phone please, Helmet, there's a good lad.

RODDY: Eh?

SAL: (*Off.*) Get the phone, I'm up a ladder!

RODDY: Oh…eh… (*Suddenly nervous. His first job. Before he picks up the phone.*) 'Hello… Good evening, The Zone, Roddy speaking…' (*Answers the phone.*) Good zone the Roddy evening. How may I help you?… Roddy… He's up a ladder… No he can't, I don't think… (*Gets a pen for the message.*) Junior…yeah…oh right…(*Listens to the details and groans.*)

RODDY slams the phone down and moves away from it as if it were a snake. His energy goes way down. He's panicking.

SAL: (*Entering holding the game.*) Who was it? Helmet? Who was it?

RODDY: Ehm…eh…no-one. Wrong number.

SAL: (*Looks at the phone.*) It wasn't man, it was Junior. These phones are wicked. The number comes up so you can see who's calling before you pick up. Great for when you can't pay the bills, know what I mean? What did you say? Did you think it was a wrong number? What's wrong with you?

RODDY: I'm sorry.

SAL: It's alright, I'll phone him back. He just wants to get on my case about the shop. Or Bindi'll be there and

they'll be having a big family meeting about my failures.
Or worse still, Dad'll be there and that rat Junior will
have grassed me in. God. Suppose I'd better phone them
back. (*He picks up the phone.*)

RODDY: No! You said we weren't going to do stuff in the
real world. You said we were going to play a game!

SAL: We will, in a minute.

RODDY: Now!

SAL: In a minute!

RODDY: I'm sorry. I'm sorry!

*RODDY loses energy and backs away towards the door. SAL
gives him a strange look and motions that he has to stay, he'll
only be a minute. SAL dials and then speaks on the phone.*

SAL: Hello. Junior man is Bindi… What's up man. (*In
Punjabi.*) No man, what? (*Horror.*) What? What? Where?
Is she alright? Orange Arch. What was she doing at
Orange Arch? Is she alright? Oh no…oh no…right. I'll
be right there. Have you phoned an ambulance? Phone
an ambulance! Is she alright? I don't care about the
bloody money, is my wife alright? I'm coming over.

*SAL puts the phone down and loses energy fast and moves
quickly into a headless chicken routine.*

(*English.*) I can't believe it. Orange Arch! What was she
thinking? If I ever… I mean what kind of monster…
Monsters! God!

*SAL disappears through the back for a second, enters with his
coat on.*

Helmet, you stay here. I'll pull the shutters down after
me and someone will come over with the keys in about
twenty minutes. Any trouble just phone the restaurant,
the number's there. Just play games we won't be long.

RODDY: *Wait!*

SAL: What?

Pause. Something in RODDY's eyes makes SAL look back at the bag of coins sitting on the counter. It takes a minute, but SAL puts two and two together. Energy down on both. SAL empties the bag of coins. There's a set of keys in it. The keys for the shutters.

RODDY: (*Quietly.*) You said we were going to play a game.

SAL: We are. But I've just completed it. I just solved it. I know how to beat it. I can get by this bit now.

RODDY: (*Nearly breaking. Putting on a very flimsy front.*) Are you going to be throwing out any games when the shop shuts?

SAL: Did you know? Did you know it was her? Did you? Did you Helmet?

A pause. A stand off. RODDY starts to cry.

RODDY: What are you going to do?

SAL looks furious but his voice is low.

SAL: I'm going to walk out that door and pull the shutters behind me. (*Holding up the keys.*) I'm going to lock the shutters and then I'm going to make sure my wife is alright. When I'm absolutely certain she's well and when I've apologised to her and to my dad, I'm coming back here.

RODDY: What…what about me?

SAL: You'll be here. You're going to stay here. And whatever happens…happens.

RODDY: What's going to happen?

SAL: *I don't know!* I don't know. But you stay here.

SAL can't even look at RODDY as he hurries out the door. RODDY's stunned. Frozen. We hear the shutters close and the shop darkens. RODDY is alone in the shop. This is what he wanted. This is his dream, but not in a nice way. Now he's a prisoner. He wanders for a bit. Touches things. Then he starts to play a game he has played before. He pretends he owns the shop. Starts to move like SAL. Goes behind the counter.

RODDY: You're so stupid, man. This is my shop. Effort and concentration. I know everything about games. Ask me anything. That's easy, Wipeout 2097. God sake, Charlie, you don't know anything. Just stand there and play the games. You've been in the shop for hours man, run about. Go out and breathe man. This is my shop.

Pause. RODDY's game hasn't worked. He can't disappear anymore. He starts to cry. And he cries on. All his energy and lives are slipping away. It seems very likely that this is the end of RODDY and of the play. But something happens. RODDY seems to sense that this is the end of him and can't accept it, in fact he's hysterical.

No, no, no...no, no... *No!*

On this last 'No!' Roddy bangs his fists on the counter and there's an extreme change in the lighting and sound as if this were all a Playstation and RODDY's given it a thump. The play has crashed. There is darkness with white noise. After a few long beats the play resumes but without the usual sound effects. Something's not quite right here. This scene should have a similar feel to the monologue; in a strange way outwith the 'game'.

9.08pm

The phone rings.

RODDY: Ha ha ha. Sal, see if you open another shop, can I work there when I'm thirty?

SAL: (*Off.*) Yes. Get the phone please, Helmet, there's a
good lad.

RODDY: Eh?

SAL: (*Off.*) Get the phone, I'm up a ladder!

*RODDY has a think about it. His energy goes down. He looks
at it as if it were a poisonous snake. After a quick glance over
his shoulder, RODDY unplugs the phone and runs back to
the console. He can't allow anything to infringe on this moment.*

(*Entering with the game.*) Did you get the phone?

RODDY: I didn't know what to do.

SAL: You didn't know what to do? You don't know…what
do they teach you in school?

*SAL puts the game in the Playstation and starts it up. He
notices RODDY's guilt.*

I wouldn't worry about it, Helmet, it'll be Junior. He'll
just want to get on my case about the shop. Or Bindi'll
be there and they'll be having a big family meeting
about my failures. Or worse still, Dad'll be there and that
rat Junior will have grassed me in. God. Well… I'm a
man of my word…they can wait. I am not at home to
reality.

*SAL goes over to the phone and takes it off the hook. Just as
he's about to return to the console he notices that the phone is
unplugged. He looks at the phone and then to RODDY who's
staring at the screen.*

RODDY: (*Quietly.*) You said we were going to play a game.

SAL: We are. Roddy…?

RODDY: I wish we could play games forever.

SAL: I know what you mean.

RODDY: I love playing games, man.

SAL: Yeah. (*Snapping out of a strange vague feeling.*) Yeah exactly. The real world can wait.

RODDY: I want to remember it exactly like this.

They're both ready to start playing. RODDY's looking round at the shop, strangely not totally hooked into the game as yet. He looks at the phone sadly. SAL catches his eye.

What's going to happen?

SAL: (*Shrugs.*) Whatever happens, happens.

RODDY: Sal? Can I tell you something.

Pause.

SAL: (*Shakes his head.*) Ssssh.

The game is loaded. RODDY smiles. He goes back to business. The lights fade like a sunset as they play.

The End.